eBay

Find All You Need to Sell on eBay and Build a Profitable Business from Scratch, Step-By-Step.

Felix Alvaro

Acknowledgments

Firstly, I want to thank God for giving me the knowledge and inspiration to put this informative book together. I also want to thank my parents, my brothers and my partner Silvia for their support.

Table of Contents

Introduction

Hi there! Congratulations on acquiring this eBook. I can see that you value and understand the importance of planning and acquiring the right information before taking on a new business venture. Few people make that decision, so well-done.

My name is Felix Alvaro and I am an Internet Marketer, Entrepreneur and Author with the mission to motivate and inspire you to achieve your goals, by sharing my knowledge and experience through my books.

Today, I am going to be passing to you all that you need to know to establish a profitable eBay business from scratch! Not only that, but I will be also giving you a bit of my mentality and point-of-view so that you are fully ready to get started.

As you may know, eBay is one of the largest online retailers in the World, going head-to-head with big names such as Amazon, Craigslist, and Etsy. Just to give you an idea, last year these retailers had a total revenue of $89.4 Billion and eBay alone took the second largest slice of the pie, a total of $17.9 Billion (Craigslist took home $335M and Etsy $195M).

"So why is this important?", you ask.

Well, this is very important because eBay doesn't actually sell the products themselves. Instead, they provide a massive platform where independent sellers (people like you and me) can offer whatever products they choose directly to eBay's *never-ending* customer-base and then simply share the profits.

Through this simple concept, thousands of sellers are earning a very comfortable living by partnering-up with eBay, and you can most definitely get a slice of this billion-dollar industry. How? You will find the answer to that question in this book. Just follow the simple steps that I am going to lay out for you in this book and you will be on your way. I will cover **all** you need to know to create your eBay store, list your items correctly and begin generating income right away.

Online businesses are the future, hence why I heavily invest my own money and time into as many lucrative online endeavours as possible. Nowadays, opening a successful, traditional bricks-and-mortar business is extremely difficult and very risky. Today only 2 out of 10 traditional businesses survive the first year, meaning that you have an 80% chance of losing. Not to be pessimistic, because risk is good, but it has to be calculated risk. That is simple not a game I am excited to play.

However, the online market is booming! Today people from all ages and backgrounds have the ability to make a killing online like never before. All they really require is the correct guidance and the right vehicle. That is why this book was created, with the aim to provide you with the guidance you need to succeed on one of the most lucrative vehicles in the World, eBay.

So, without further ado, let's begin...

In the first chapter, I will briefly tell you a little bit more about eBay and why **you need** to be selling on their store, before moving onto the real-meat of this book in the following chapters...

Chapter One: Why You Need To Be Selling on EBay

In this first chapter, I will briefly discuss a few reasons why you need to be selling on eBay, why it is a great platform and what advantages this platform can bring to someone like you, who is also interested in starting an online business.

EBay is a very successful marketplace, and better than that, it also makes many of their independent sellers very successful. A huge reason for this is the fact that they allow sellers to build their own businesses in their own unique way. Here are a few points to give you a better understanding:

Seller Flexibility

When selling your item on eBay, eBay acts as a medium between the buyer and you the seller. Through this partnership, you are able to achieve global market success using a platform that is already well-established.

EBay doesn't really dictate what to, or what not to do with your own store, thus giving you the advantage to customize it and make it look how you want, and reach the buyers you want to target. For example, on eBay, sellers are allowed to set their own shipping fees as well as their own returns policies, if any.

As a seller, you have the freedom to upload photos of your choice and write your own products descriptions for your listing. This allows the seller to be creative and to build an online business that is theirs and not built around someone else's ideas.

You Can Brand Your Store

This goes hand-in-hand with the point I just covered previously. EBay wants you to use their platform to build a brand-image, and according to eBay's officials, it's easy to do so. For example, you can create and add a logo, create a billboard for your store, choose which products to get highlighted when the store gets a visit, ask consumers to sign up for your newsletter, as well as let customers network with your store's social media platforms at the click of a mouse!

We will go into more detail about how to brand effectively in a later chapter, so definitely stick around for that.

Global Markets

On eBay, you are able to connect to an average of thirty countries, allowing you to connect with over 150 million buyers. In fact, 98 percent of eBay's current commercial sellers already export within these 30 countries, giving eBay (and you) an advantage against other companies that only operate in a much smaller market.

Also, eBay has a global shipping program that makes it easy to export items to customers all over the world, increasing your chances of success by allowing you to reach markets you would otherwise be unable to reach.

No Limit Selling On eBay

Finally, unlike other online marketplaces that have a central directory of products to be posted for sale, eBay has no limit on what you can sell. In fact, there are no tough restrictions on what type of products you should or should not sell on eBay (apart from obvious ones like alcohol and tobacco and a few others listed here: http://pages.ebay.com/help/policies/items-ov.html#prohibited).

On eBay, you have the freedom to sell anything from handcrafted items, to vintage products or anything unique that you choose to. That means that no matter your product category, you are able to offer that to buyers from a large pool of potential customers from all around the world, increase your chances of success many times over.

I hope this chapter has showed you the potential that there is with eBay. I believe many people are reluctant to start with a big platform like eBay, because they expect a lot of control with no room for creativity and expression, but as you have just learned, that is definitely not the case. EBay allows flexibility, encourages branding, and places a global market in your hands, making it so much easier to achieve your financial goals.

In the next chapter, I will take you through the first few steps you need to take to get your business up and running correctly, as well as the different ways you can get paid. I have made the steps very simple and have also included a few images to make it even easier to follow along. So, stay tuned…

Chapter Two: Getting Started

Now that you understand how eBay operates, and understand the vision they have for you as a seller, it is now time to move on to some practical steps you must complete to get started. In this chapter, you will learn how to open up your online store, as well as how the payment and selling process works.

No waffling around, time is money. Here are some important steps that you need to take to get your business on the map;

Step One: Decide the Type of Account Suitable For You

Your first decision should be to whether operate using a business eBay account, or simply use your own personal private eBay account (assuming you already have one). Sincerely, making this decision should not be very hard, as there are some major differences in the two accounts that can have an impact in how you operate and I will break those down for you now.

Firstly, the private/personal account is more suitable for people that are customers of eBay and that may want to sell some of their unwanted items a few times a year. The account should not be used by people that are buying and reselling items, which if you are reading this book, it is highly likely what you are looking to do.

However, on the bright-side, the fee structure eBay has put in place is much simpler with a personal account, with a flat rate fee of 10% (this is what eBay will charge once the item has sold and it excludes media and technology products) plus a small PayPal transaction fee. (Find more about fees here: http://pages.ebay.com/help/sell/fees.html).

The business account, on the other-hand, is more suitable for you and me. This account is for people looking to start an online business to sell a large number of products on a constant basis. In terms of the seller fees, some product categories do come with fees slightly higher than 10% but the majority are actually much less than that.

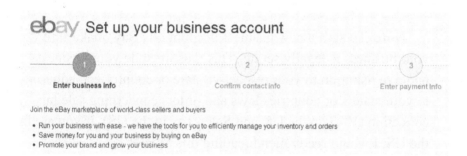

Some other key benefits of the business account include;

- Receive your invoices set as NET, which allows you to claim back your sales tax (VAT in the UK). This can make a huge impact on your net profits at the end of the year.

- Allows you to provide buyers with contact information, which will increase your credibility and trust from new customers, and therefore likely boost your sales.
- Allows you to create a Terms & Conditions and a Returns Policy for your store, which will again be increasing your customers' confidence in your store and your products. T&C's and returns are very important; we will talk more about that in the upcoming chapters.
- You will receive a 'Business Seller' classification so that buyers can differentiate between you (a business) from a random person selling items online. This will motivate more people to buy from you, as it is easier to trust someone that is a registered and verified seller, instead of an unknown individual.

Note: To start a new business account on eBay, make sure your business is legally set up. This must include your business name registration to your respective state or country and adhering to your state's or countries laws and orders concerning sale tax collection (VAT in the UK and Sales Tax in the US). If you are in the US, I would recommend reading this article: http://www.entrepreneur.com/article/79562 to get more information on this topic. If you live in the UK, you will have to register as self-employed (within 3 months) and pay Type 2 National Insurance contributions and income tax. Visit: https://www.gov.uk/working-for-yourself/what-counts-as-self-employed for more details on that.

Step Two: Choose a Username

When choosing a user name for your account, you should consider a name that won't be seen as offensive or cause negative connotations. I know that sounds like common-sense, but surprisingly a lot of sellers actually make this mistake. More importantly, be sure to pick a username that is suitable to your market and audience. This could be including a keyword that matches what your customers would be searching for and of course, the name of your business.

Now, while choosing a good eBay username is an important task, don't get too caught up in finding the 'perfect' username. I say this because once you've opened your eBay account, the platform allows you to change your user name later without losing critical data.

Step Three: Set up a PayPal Account

For you to receive your payment after selling on eBay, you'll be required to have a PayPal account. In fact, PayPal is the most convenient and reliable option for you, especially from your customer's point of view. PayPal gives buyers a little bit more peace-of-mind when shopping online because they offer a very secure service, that guarantees buyers their money back if there are any complications with their order.

Sign up for free.

Choose from 2 types of accounts:

○ Personal Account

Shop, receive money, or just pay someone back for lunch. All without sharing your payment info.

◉ Business Account

Accept all major credit cards online or at the register. Send secure invoices to your customers.

See for yourself why 169 million people love PayPal

Continue

Similar to eBay, PayPal has different types of accounts you can open with them. The three accounts are; *Personal Account*, *Business standard Account* (or Premier Accounts) and finally the *Business Pro Account*. With the *Personal* account, you can pay for things and you can also receive payments from people. However, similar to eBay, it is quite limiting and not ideal for a business (doesn't even allow credit card transactions).

That is unless you upgrade it, which I will show you how to do shortly.

Then there is the *Business Standard account*, which is ideal for sellers who want to get paid online (credit card transactions are accepted!) and also make online purchases. Finally, there is the *Business Pro* account, which is for larger scale operations. With the Pro account, you get features like multi-user access,

16

which allows up to 200 employees to use the same account, you can also display your logo and business name on the check-out page for more professionalism and better branding.

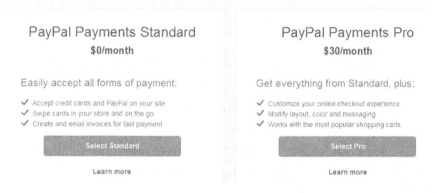

My recommendation is to always go with the Business Standard account. It is free and will still allow you to benefit from PayPal's secure and reputable service. To open your account, follow the following steps;

1. Visit the PayPal website (paypal.com)
2. Click *Sign-up* on the top right of the page
3. Select *Business Account* and click *Continue*
4. Click *Select Standard*
5. Fill in your information...
6. Read through the PayPal policies and select *Agree and Continue*

7. Then you want to verify your account (highly recommended) by adding your banking information- PayPal will then deposit a particular amount of money in your account within 3 days, you then have to simply enter the exact figure that was deposited in the *Verifications* section of the account.

To upgrade your Private account, follow these simple steps:

1. Visit your *Account Overview* page
2. Click on *Upgrade* link
3. You should be given the option of a Premier or Business account. Select whichever you prefer
4. Click *Upgrade Now* and then click *Continue* and that should be done!

Step Four: Plan Ahead!

Even though the online market is booming, you still have to treat your eBay business like a real business (which it is) and give it all the dedication it requires. This means having a direction for your business, and having goals to keep you on track. Ask yourself;

"What exactly do I want to achieve with eBay"?

"How many hours am I willing to put in every-week to achieve that goal?"

"By what date do I want to achieve it?"

"What is my strategy to attain my goal?"

Thinking like this will put you ahead of 95% of sellers, who jump in with closed eyes, with no idea what they want from eBay, and just 'hope' they make money. Don't be like those people, be like the 5% that create massive success.

You don't have to write a 5000-word business plan, just get out a pen and paper and answer the questions I have just told you. Put them up on the wall if you have to and look at them every-day. It will remind why you are doing this, what you have to do and how you have to do it.

EBay's Payment Structure

Now onto the money side of things. As far as we know, PayPal is eBay's preferred mode of payment and the benefits are pretty clear. However, as a seller, there are a few payment options you can offer your buyers;

- **PayPal**- Fastest and most convenient method of payment for both parties.

- **PayPal Credit** (ebay.com)- PayPal's own credit line that allows buyers to pay for items and then pay PayPal monthly.
- **Credit/Debit Card**- Credit card transaction without using PayPal, you will require a merchant account for this.
- **Payment on-collection**- If you want to deliver the product and collect the payment in person
- **Skrill** (ebay.com)- Online money transfers. Contact (merchantservices@skrill.com) to receive payments using this service
- **Cheque** or **Postal order**- Give the buyer the option to post a cheque out to you (Restricted to certain categories on ebay.com)
- **Escrow** (ebay.co.uk and ebay.ie)- Payments for pricier items where the escrow service provider holds the buyer's payment until the item is received.

Bear in mind that eBay does not exactly dictate which form of payment buyers should use while making purchases, however, be aware that PayPal payments are the only payment method under eBay's *Buyer Protection Policy*. Again, the benefits are clear for both the buyer and the seller; speed, security and convenience, so try to use that method as much as possible.

Note: When a buyer pays using their bank account balance and not their PayPal balance, it takes anywhere between 4-7 days for PayPal to clear the payment and feature that payment in the seller's account. So, bear that in mind.

I will now lay out for you the **payment structure** so you know exactly how you will get paid. I will also provide you with some advice on what to do if a customer does not pay for their item.

Step One- Product Purchase

When a buyer makes a purchase on your listing, be it a "buy it now" item or an auction, eBay will automatically generate a notice for both the buyer and yourself.

Step Two- Send Invoice/Note (auction items)

If your listing is an auction, eBay will also send the winning bidder an invoice notification. If your customer does not make the payment immediately, or you want to also send them an invoice, then from your eBay page scroll, click *Action* and then you can send an invoice. It will also allow you to add a note to the buyer such as "Please complete your payments within x working days'.

Step Three- Payment Complete

Once a buyer has completed their purchase and paid for the item using PayPal, they will immediately receive a transaction confirmation email. You, the seller, will also be notified, and on the eBay page you'll see the *paid* icon.

Step Four- Receiving Funds

- If the payment was done via **PayPal** or **PayPal Credits**, in most cases, the money will be transferred to your PayPal account immediately.
- For **Credit Card** payments, your merchant account should be credited as soon as the buyer's bank-card is processed and payment accepted.
- With Payment on **Collection,** the payment is received in-person as you deliver the item.
- With **Skrill** you get an instant online transfer to your Skrill account
- **Cheques** vary according to your bank or building society. The funds usually become available in your account within 4-7 working-days from the day the cheque is deposited.
- With **Escrow** services, the payment is transferred to the seller once the buyer receives the item and reports that everything is okay.

Step Five- Unpaid Items

In some cases, buyers don't actually go-ahead with the transactions, which is where you can use the 'Contact Buyer' form to reach-out to the buyer once more. If that doesn't work, then you can contact *eBay's Resolution Centre*. By doing so, eBay is able to generate a message to that buyer which helps the seller avoid paying final item fees that are charged by eBay after a product sale.

Great stuff! In this chapter, you have learned about the different account options you have with eBay and PayPal, you also learned about the payment structure, the different payment methods you have available, and how to set everything up.

The next chapter is very important, as I will teach you how to know which products are in demand, as well as where to source the best products from. If you don't find a profitable niche or market that is already making money, then everything else won't matter. This information is crucial, so stay tuned. Great progress so far…

Chapter Three: Selling Product People Want to Buy

In this chapter, we will discuss the very important task of finding the most profitable, in-demand products and the best places to source them from. Selling products people actually want, and selling them for a profit, is the only way you can succeed in any business endeavour, so pay close attention to what I am about to show you...

Find High-in-Demand Products

There are a few ways you can find out what to sell on eBay. I will provide you a few great sources and ideas that you can use to get started. A lot of people believe that you have to create something new and amazing to be successful online. They think there's too much competition in the profitable markets and that it is impossible to get a slice of the pie. That is inaccurate, you don't have to try and reinvent the wheel to make money online.

As a matter-of-fact, it is the exact opposite. Like I mentioned at the end of the last chapter, you need the competition to show you what is selling well and what is not. All you then do is think

24

of ways in which you can beat them, for example; better branding, marketing, quality, customer service and higher ranking.

One of my favourite ways to find products that are selling well, is by visiting *Amazon's Best Seller* list. EBay used to have a *What's Hot* list, but that was probably giving it all away. However, the Amazon list is just as good if not better. All you do is go to Google and search 'Amazon Best Seller' or visit: http://www.amazon.com/best-sellers/zgbs. Once you are on the list, you will see a huge number of categories that you can choose from on the left-hand side.

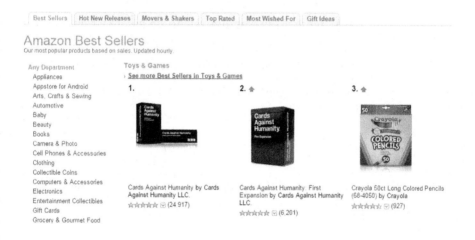

Before I teach you the steps to take when analysing Amazon's list, I would advise you to look for products that meet the following criteria;

- Are not too big or heavy- Larger and heavier items are more expensive to ship to customers, therefore reducing your profit margin.
- Don't cost less than $10- You will narrow your profit margin too much when you take into account the shipping fees + supplier's fees + eBay's fees. You want to go for a product that has a good profit margin.
- With that being said, don't go for anything that costs more than $40- If a product sells on eBay for $50, it will probably cost you $20 to make, making your initial investment quite high and also increasing your risk.
- I would avoid electronics or products that people consume when you are first starting out- It is very risky, have a few regulations to be aware of and also you run the risk of getting many returns, complaints and bad reviews, especially with electronics.
- Go for something light, that is easy to make and dispatch!

Once you have taken the above into account, you want to do the following:

1. Select a category that catches your attention and that you generally have some interest in
2. Narrow that category down to something even-more specific (for example, choose 'Sports & Outdoors' and then narrow it down to 'Sport & Fitness', then 'Exercise

& Fitness' and then 'Cardio Training' to get to a really niche market).

3. Look through the best-selling products in that category and look for something that appeals to you and most importantly, matches the criteria I gave previously.

4. Once you have decided on a product, open-it and write down the *Amazon Best Seller Rank* and the main keyword in the title.

Here's a great product. Its light and costs between $15-$35 on Amazon:

Tone Fitness Stability Ball
by Tone Fitness
★★★★☆ ▾ 614 customer reviews | 15 answered questions

List Price: $19.99
Price: $15.12 & **FREE Shipping** on orders over $35. Details
You Save: $4.87 (24%)

In Stock
Ships from and sold by Amazon.com.

Want it tomorrow, Sept. 24? Order within 31 mins and choose One-Day
Details

Size:
55-centimeter ▾

Color: **Fuchsia**

Has a best-seller ranking of 3,541:

(The best-seller ranking gives us an idea of how well the product is doing out of all the products in that category. The previous product is ranked as the 3,541st best product in the *'Sports & Outdoors'* category, which is really good assuming there probably are hundreds of thousands of products just in that category. The **smaller** the number the better and, as a rule of thumb I tend to go for categories where the majority of the top products have a best seller ranking of 50,000 or less).

5. Then you want to identify the main keyword for this product in the title, which is basically the keyword people are most likely to search. If you take another look at the listing I showed previously, the title reads *'Tone Fitness Stability Ball'*, the keyword is *'Stability Ball'*, 'Tone Fitness' is just the brand.

6. Then we want to search that keyword on Amazon, go through the listings on the first couple of pages and again, ensure that the majority of products under this keyword (in this example: stability balls) are selling. By analysing the listings, I can get a good idea of the popularity and how well those products are doing. If the first 2 pages of products are all selling well (ranking below 50,000) that is great. If the pages after that are also selling, then you have

found a very profitable niche! If not, just move onto another product until you find a product that is:

- Light and not too big
- Between $10-$40
- Preferably not an electronic nor a product you consume
- Low Rank number
- Majority of the products in that category are selling well

Doing that exercise should give you some ideas for some great profitable markets and niches.

Another very simple task you can do is to sit down with a pen, a piece of paper and write down what you think is popular right-now and what also interests you at the moment. Look around you, look at what people are talking about, look at what you have bought lately or want to buy. Aim to write-down at least 10 ideas, no matter how 'silly' they may sound.

Once you have done that, you want to verify the success of those items, and one way is through keyword research. There are a few tools you can use that will show you the popularity of certain keywords and will also show you how competitive they are. Probably the most used free tool is the *Google AdWords Keyword Planner*.

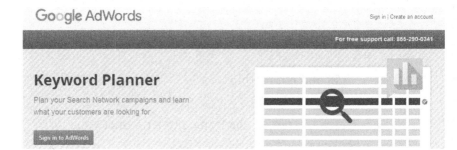

This tool will let you search particular keywords related to what you want to sell and will show how many searches are done for that particular word on a monthly basis. You can also change certain demographics of the results if you want to target a more specific market, from a particular location.

Even better than showing you the results of your keyword, it will also give you alternative results for other related keywords, therefore allowing you to know which words are more commonly used. (this is very important for writing the descriptions and titles as we will discuss in the next chapter). Simply enter all your ideas into this tool to get an idea of how large the markets are, their popularity, whether it is growing, stagnant or falling.

You can also subscribe, for a small fee, to a service called *eBay Marketplace Research.*

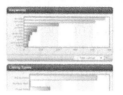

This tool alone can possibly provide you with all the information you ever need. It will reveal some valuable information about buying trends, the most popular categories, and also products that are not doing so well. (To find out more visit: http://pages.ebay.com/marketplace_research/). All this information put together, will most certainly give you an idea of popular products, allow you to verify the popularity of items you were considering and best of all, it can provoke ideas and niches of products you haven't thought about yet.

Once you believe that you have found something that is profitable using the methods I have explained, do a few more web-searches to give you that confidence and then go for it immediately! Don't wait until you are 100% convinced, or know everything about the market to take action, because one; that will probably never happen and two; even if it does, by then you may have lost momentum or lost a massive chance to succeed.

Don't be the person that suffers from 'Analysis Paralysis', where they want to know everything about something before making the decision to take action. If you are like this, you may lose a lot of great opportunities.

For me, the best time to act is when you know about 40-70% about something. 100% is too late and usually never comes. I have heard from many highly-successful people that 'Speed of Implementation' is one of the most important factors in business.

Of course, always plan and analyse your risks. Don't jump in blind-folded. Calculate your risks, know what you need to know to make a decision and go ahead.

Find a Reliable Supplier

Now that you have brainstormed and verified the popularity and demand of your products, lets now talk about where you can actually source those from;

Buying low and selling high is the simple money-making formula of every successful businessperson. The ability to buy cheap is crucial because once you sell high, the profit margins are higher (the surplus you make). If your plan is to buy new products for resale, then your products source must include manufacturers, wholesalers, sales agents, importers, liquidators, and distributers.

Deciding who to buy your products from, will often be based on your specific needs, and will be determined by the price of the product, reliability of the supplier, quality of the product, guarantee of the product from the supplier, the supplier's terms, and fulfilment. For example, if you don't have enough storage space or suitable transport, you should consider a reliable drop shipper who can deliver your items directly to your customers for you. Drop-shipping is huge, so I have dedicated a section about that in the next couple of chapters!

Now, when it comes to buying previously owned items for resale, things become slightly different but much easier. In that category of products there are no manufacturers, sales agents or wholesalers to supply cheap resale products. Instead, you will need to rely on your ability to detect bargains and your skills to negotiate the best products to purchase at a cheap price. You can find these types of items at auctions, from private sellers, from online marketplaces, thrift shops, garage sale, flea markets or even liquidators which I will discuss more in a shortly.

My personal preference is new products. I don't really like owning second hand products so it doesn't really excite me. However, what I like or don't like is not really relevant. If you know a hot market that really wants a product and you believe you know how to reach that niche, go ahead. Give that market what it wants, just ensure that you work out all your costs and start with a small investment. Test that market before you jump in head-first.

Below are some of the places where you will find products to sell on eBay, as well as some examples of actual companies and suppliers;

#1: Buy at Wholesalers

When buying new, bulky products for resale, your first option should be wholesalers. A wholesaler is a great source because they offer a broader range of goods and items than importers and manufacturers. The most common wholesalers are General merchandise suppliers. These wholesalers stock and sell different varieties of household items and products. There are other wholesalers dealing with industry specifics tools and equipment, food wholesalers, clothing and textile wholesalers, etc.

When buying from wholesalers there are no tricks. The whole process is simple because you only need to find the wholesaler who deals with the type of item you want, open an account and you are ready to buy at wholesale. Make sure to also double-check the minimum order. In most cases you can actually negotiate that down. It is always wise to start with just a few orders to test out the product and get a feel for the quality. Another tip is to always go with high rated sellers. Don't try to take huge risks and order 1,000 items from an unverified source, especially when starting out.

If you know exactly what product you want to sell (which you absolutely should!), look for wholesalers that wholesale those particular goods. For instance, if you want to sell handbags on

34

eBay you could get a great start by Google searching as many variations of the following terms;

- "Handbag wholesaler". The most obvious one
- 'Handbag distributor"
- 'Handbag wholesale distributor"
- 'Handbag dropship"
- 'Handbag wholesale dropshipper"
- 'Handbag reseller"
- 'Handbag bulk"
- 'Handbag warehouse"
- 'Handbag supplier"
- 'Handbag wholesale supplier"
- Etc...

Be sure to go deep in the search results and go through various sites and save/bookmark the best ones. Look for reviews for the wholesalers and do your due diligence to avoid scammers.

Besides using Google, you can also look through wholesaler directories where you can find numerous wholesalers that offer a variety of products. A great place to start is http://www.worldwidebrands.com/, They are reputable for providing links to great wholesalers and dropshippers, however, it is still very wise to be cautious.

#2: The Importer

With prices as low as the wholesaler, the importers are another reliable source of items you can list on eBay. They normally deal with specific products, however, there are those who deal in general merchandise. Buying from importers is similar to buying from wholesalers, and you should be able to find multiple sources all over the internet.

A very popular source of importers is Alibaba.com, which is the world's largest business-to-business and goods trading platform, with the aim to connect suppliers from all around the World, to people like you and me.

They are hands-down my favourite source because you can find suppliers from all-over the world, huge variety of products and at a great price. However, you have to take a few precautions when using their website. Firstly, **always** tick: 'Gold Supplier' and 'Assessed Supplier'.

Never buy from anyone else, period. Because everyone else is basically 'unverified' or not highly rated, so you run the risk of being scammed or dealing with a terrible supplier who will send you damaged goods, send them late, complicate orders and all sorts of issues. My advice is stay-away. That's all you really need to be cautious about with Alibaba, but if you want more details Read This: https://www.shopify.co.uk/blog/16665772-alibaba-101-how-to-safely-source-products-from-the-worlds-biggest-supplier-directory

Quick Tip: You will notice that suppliers have 'minimum orders' you must make. However, 9/10 this can be negotiated, as well as the price. My tip is **Always Negotiate**! -on both the number of items you want and the price.

#3: Buy From Liquidators

Although liquidators are like other sources, they don't deal with or stock the same product all the time. They purchase different items from different sources that include retailers unloading out-of-season goods, slow moving stock, bankrupt wholesalers, manufacturers, and distributors. Purchasing from liquidators has no limits, because of the variety of products, such as electronics, clothing, sporting goods, books, toys, low-priced items and kitchen accessories to name a few. Most items you find at liquidators are often new.

However, some may be out of season products, store returns, damaged slightly or discontinued. Again bear-in-mind that if you want to continuously sell one range of products, they may not be the best source, because the stock of that product is limited to what they received. You can find liquidators online or at large auction events. Again, check reviews if buying online and always pay with PayPal.

#4: Buy From The Factory

The last one I will mention is buying directly from the factory. With the help of the internet, it's easy to source manufacturers and buy directly from them anywhere globally, cutting out the middle-man and giving you a better price, more reliability, guaranteed quality and satisfaction. You can also find their products in the manufacturer's own outlet stores (if they have any), just be sure to have all the information of the exact products you want. Also keep-in-mind that you must have space to store your goods.

Retail Arbitrage

Retail Arbitrage is buying something from one place and then turning around and immediately selling it in another place. It can include any type of item such as jewelry, books, toys, clothes, accessories, gold, foreign money, and so much more. This probably the easiest way to get started selling on eBay.

You can sell your old items or buy cheap products that you can flip. This is how most successful sellers start. You don't have to go all out with big orders from wholesalers and huge stocks, you can simply visit yard sales, charity shops, thrift stores etc and grab some good deals.

The only downfall with Retail Arbitrage is that you have to continuously go out there and source products to flip, and you have to also deal with shipping, packaging, labelling and so on. However, this should not demotivate you as this can be a great way to begin making money online. So, whether you want just some additional cash or a full- time income, those are both very achievable with Retail Arbitrage on eBay.

The process of using a retail arbitrage store works very easily; you set up your store on eBay how we broke it down in Chapter 2 and begin going out there looking for some good deals to flip.

The big question is what do you sell and how do you know if it's a good deal?

When you come across an item which you believe is undervalued, you want to check eBay and see what the item has been selling for, as well as the *Sell Through Rate* (STR) for an item you want to sell (STR is the number of listings of a particular product minus the number of items that actually sold).

You can find the STR by searching the item you want (be very specific), under *'Show Only'* click on *'Sold Listings'* to see how many items sold and then click on *'Completed Listings'* to see the total number of listings and then you divide the number of sold auctions buy the number of completed listings and that should give you a percentage (For example: 5614 sold auctions / 15753 completed listings = 0.356 which is 36%). That means that 36% of the listings for that particular product got sold. You want items with the highest STRs possible, as relisting items can increase your eBay fees and decrease your profit margin. I wouldn't sell products that have a STR below 60%.

You can also use apps like *'What's it worth on eBay?'* (by Twofingers Apps), to get a quick average sold price for your item.

What's it worth on eBay? FREE

Twofingers Apps   Shopping   ★ ★ ★ ★ 2,941 👤

🔲 PEGI 3

ⓘ This app is compatible with all of your devices.

☑ Added to Wishlist

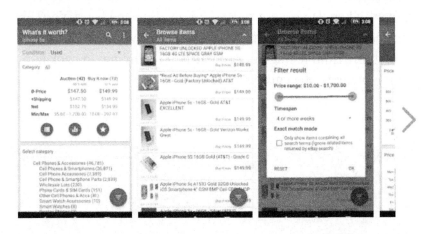

What's it worth on eBay? That's what you want to know before selling your stuff on eBay or anywhere else. The eValuator app determines a realistic average price from items successfully sold in the past weeks.

This way you can quickly know whether you are getting a good deal or not, and are able to make a profit.

REMEMBER: You have to always take shipping, packaging, eBay fees and PayPal fees into account. These costs change often, so check eBay and PayPal for the latest fees. Have an idea of what kind of margin is worth it for you so that you focus on products that will make you enough profit.

When sourcing your products, make sure to check the product thoroughly. Make sure everything is in place, and that you have every part. If its clothes, inspect the quality and look out for replicas. A great guy to follow to get ideas on what products do well and to just overall know how the eBay game works, is Steve Raiken. He is very successful on eBay and has a YouTube channel called 'Raiken Profit'. He will give you a lot of tips on everything from listing your products, to sourcing, to packaging, taking pictures, the entire process.

Raiken Profit

Home   Videos   Playlists   Channels   Discussion   About

What to watch next

How Much Money Can You Really Make On Ebay?
by Raiken Profit
2,957 views 1 day ago

Studying The Sold Listings On Ebay - Researching Ho...
by Raiken Profit
2,451 views 4 days ago

What To Sell On Amazon FBA - 11 Items I Sold In M...
by Raiken Profit
2,490 views 5 days ago

10 Top Selling Clothing Items To Sell In Your Ebay

Fantastic. Now that you have learned how to find products that people want to buy and know where to find quality supplier, it's now time to move on to actually selling. The beauty about an online business is that once you have created your 'pitch' -or in this case your listing- and you do it right, you don't really have to do it again. Of course, there are some key areas you have to focus on, which is what we are going to talk about in this up-coming chapter...

Chapter Four: Your First Listing

Now that we have a great product and an awesome supplier, let's talk about your first listing. In this chapter, I will cover some key areas that you should focus-on to correctly list you items and in result, boost your sales. Let's begin!

Categories

The categories are a great way by which people can find products they are looking for, so you have to make sure that you select a category that is relevant to your listing. You can also choose additional categories for a small fee and this will help increase the number of people that see your listing. An important, but simple step.

Title and Description-

The title and the description are very important, as they can literally make or break you. The title has to be both eye-catching and at the same time, keyword and search result optimized. With the title, ensure that it contains the main keyword that people would search for, when searching for your product.

Here is a simple example just for illustration purposes:

I am selling a pair of used Nike Jordan trainers. For the title, I have chosen; *"Nike Air Jordan Retro 6 Infrared White- Size 8 RRP: £140"*.

Tell us what you're selling

Nike Air Jordan Retro 6 Infrared White- Size 8 RRP: £140

e.g. Men's blue Adidas Glide running shoes size 11 | You can also enter the UPC or ISBN of your item 🕦

Se

As you can see from that title, I have started with the main keywords which are 'Nike Air Jordan'. This is what the customer is most likely to search, or even 'Jordan 6'. I have also included the colour, size and the original price of the product which makes the listing look like a bargain and a good price.

Now, as this is 1 used item and also a one-off sale, some of the things I have included in the title may not be suitable for a product that you are selling more than one, or different sizes, colours etc. If I had more stock of this product, with different colours and sizes, my title could be something like; *"Nike Air Jordan Retro 6, Sizes 5-10 RRP: £140"*.

If you used the Google AdWords tool, you should by now have an idea of which keywords and terms are the best for your products. For instance, if you are selling headphones, include the word 'earphones', 'headphones', 'headset' -or whichever is most popular- in your title. Ensure that you use the 60-80 characters to push you up at the top of the search results in the easiest way possible.

The description also needs to be engaging, descriptive and keyword optimized. Make sure to include as many keywords as you can, be very detailed, and mention all the key features and benefits of your item, as this will prevent you having to waste time answering basic questions about the product. I would recommend 250-300 words for the description and also don't forget to spell-check everything. If you are familiar with HTML, you can also create a better and more attractive description.

For the same listing, here is the description I used:

Nike Air Jordan Retro 6 Infrared White- Size 8 RRP: £140

This is a really cool and 100% Authentic pair of Nike Air Jordan Retro 6's which I am selling since I don't wear them at all. Purchased from the NIKE Store in Stratford- RRP: £140

They are in excellent condition as were only worn a couple of times and have been thoroughly cleaned. The only signs of wear are some barely visible lines on the back of the shoe and a tiny spec on the front left shoe.

Men's UK Size 8 (US 9)

Grab this bargain price now before it's gone!

Thank you

Which reads:

"Nike Air Jordan Retro 6 Infrared White- Size 8 RRP: £140

This is a really cool and **100% Authentic** pair of Nike Air Jordan Retro 6's which I am selling since I don't wear them at all. Purchased from the NIKE Store in Stratford- **RRP: £140**

They are in excellent condition as were only worn a couple of times and have been thoroughly cleaned. The only signs of wear are some barely visible lines on the back of the shoe and a tiny spec on the front left shoe.

Men's **UK Size 8** (US 9)

Grab this bargain price now before it's gone!

Thank you"

As you can see from the description, I explain what the item is in detail, I give a reason why I am selling (for used items, if people don't know why you are selling they make think the item is damaged, stolen etc.).

I tell them about any faults with the item, use buzz words (ex: excellent, fantastic, amazing...) and end with a call-to-action. The call to action is vital, as it urges the customer to buy and also gives little fear of loss.

Note: This is just an example of a one-time sale of a used item, if you are building a brand, you need to be even more descriptive and have a better presentation. Use Header tags (HTML), your logo if you have one etc.

Besides the description, eBay also lets you add more '*Item Specifics*' where you can add additional information about the product. I strongly recommend you do this as it will only benefit you and increase your chances of making sales. For my Jordan trainers, here is what I added:

* Item specifics ⓘ

* Shoe Size		* Brand	
UK 8	▼	Jordan	▼

More item specifics

Style		EU Shoe Size	
Trainers	▼	42	▼

Main Colour		Upper Material	
White	▼	100% Leather	▼

Lining		Sole	
	▼		▼

Product ID		MPN	
	▼		▼

Country/Region of Manufacture	
	▼

Listing Images

Together with the title and description, the picture is with no-doubt one of the most important parts of the listing. For you to sell on eBay, you must use a picture that will make your listing stand out and attract buyers, it's that simple. About 85% of eBay shoppers will skip imageless auctions, and many others will also ignore listings will low quality or grainy images. Using just any picture is not enough, so avoid "stock images" as they also don't work.

Simply take photos with a high- quality camera, in a well-lit place, possibly on a white background and get as many shots as you can to compare with. Depending on your category, you want to have a minimum of 5 high-quality images. EBay will let you post a maximum of 12 images for free. I would recommend using as close to 12 as possible. This shows credibility, and makes the customer more likely to purchase from you.

Note: If you are selling used items, make sure to also include photos of any faults of defects of the product.

Shipping Costs

With shipping, you can use eBay's own shipping calculator to work out your shipping costs. When filling in the selling form, you should see a section called *'Add Shipping details'*. There you want to choose *'Calculated: Cost Varies By Buyer Location'*. This will set the price for each individual customer according to their location. You then want to select a package type, (visit: http://pages.ebay.com/help/pay/package-sizes.html for package types) followed by the weight, and up-to 3 shipping services you want to use. Finally, it will ask you if you want to add any handling costs. Personally, I would not charge anything more here unless you really do have genuine high costs of packaging and handling.

With popular items, like the Nike trainers I am using in this example, eBay will actually provide you with an estimated delivery cost based on the common weight of the item and the postage price of similar items. If your items are very light or if your margins are really good (which I hope!), you can even offer free delivery. This will really set you apart from other sellers as many shoppers (like myself lol!) hate paying for delivery. Think about this and calculate whether you can afford it and whether it is worth it for your market.

Select postage for me | Select postage myself | Offer local collection or

We'll apply this option based on how similar items were posted. Learn more

Royal Mail 1st Class (1 working day) — Medium Parcel — 2kg
Estimated postage cost: **£8.90**

☐ Offer free P&P

☐ Offer local collection

Pricing

It is crucial to know about the pricing of a product before deciding to sell it. This is where I would say "you need to know everything. All your costs, such as packaging, shipping, storage, and the price it will cost you to buy it, and deduct that from the price customers will pay, to work-out your profits.

To know the best prices, just look at your competition. Search on eBay itself, look at closed auctions to see what people paid for it, look at *Buy It Now* prices and also take a look on other online stores to know what people are paying. Knowing your competitor's price is key, as it will reveal to you how your type of item is performing on the market, and also prevent you from charging too much or too little for your products.

Do your research and also bear-in-mind that majority of people that visit eBay are looking for a good price. I would recommend selling at the lowest price (whilst making some profit after expenses) at least for the beginning where you mostly want to focus on your brand, giving great service, building trust from your customers and getting positive feedback.

To help, eBay will provide you a recommended price. This recommended price is what they believe the product will sell best at, as they match it against similar products and what they have sold for. This can actually be a good indication of whether you are pricing your item correctly. They will even provide you with the price range you item has sold for before.

Tip: Similar items sold between £67.00 and £132.00.

EBay also has a feature called '*Best Offer*' where customers are able to send you offers on what they would be happy to pay for your item. If you accept their offer, the listing will end and the item will be sold. You can remove this feature by simply unticking the '*Add Best Offer*' box in the '*Price*' section.

TIP: A brilliant feature that eBay has that I will quickly mention is the Automatic relist. For a fee, eBay will relist your item if it doesn't sell during the original listing period.

Terms and Conditions/Returns

Like I mentioned before, it is highly advisable, if not mandatory to always include a Terms and Conditions policy on every listing. All the information you really need is:

1. Payment methods you accept
2. Your Returns Policy -whether you want to accept returns/exchanges (also recommended but depending on your category)
3. Shipping costs and delivery method
4. Any relevant Taxes/government fees

5. Explain the terms of the transaction

Note: Be sure to abide by what you write in the T's and C's. For example, if you say you accept returns, make sure to accept them no-matter what as eBay does not take that lightly. Be wise and fair.

(Read more about this here: http://sellercentre.ebay.co.uk/selling-practices-policy#terms)

Reply To All Questions

Even though I recommended you be very descriptive, to avoid receiving basic questions, you will still receive a number of queries from customers seeking more information about your product. Of course, that can be a good indication that people are actually interested in your products.

Be sure to regularly check your eBay account, as well as your emails, at least three times a day and answer consumers' concerns immediately. Regardless of how small the question may seem, reply in a prompt and courteous manner ensuring to answer all the user's questions to the best of your knowledge.

TIP: If you get asked the same question by many users, post the response publicly.

Pay Attention to EBay's Fee Structure and Listing Guidelines

Besides the tips I gave you previously, it is still very wise to not ignore eBay's fees structures and most importantly, the listing guidelines. I have given you an advantage by teaching you about keyword optimization and so on but be sure to not abuse it. There are guidelines that you should not cross when creating your first listing. Just to provide you with a bit more information, I have attached a great link http://pages.ebay.com/help/policies/search-manipulation.html

And another here: http://sellercentre.ebay.co.uk/selling-practices-policy

In this chapter, you have learned how to successfully create a listing that is both attractive to buyers and optimized for search results. In the next chapter, I will show you how to correctly market your business to get maximum exposure and therefore maximize your revenue.

Let's move on!

Chapter Five: Getting Your Products in-front of Your Customer-base

In this chapter, we are going to move onto a very key area of any business: marketing. The way you market your business and the ability that you have to get your product in-front of your customers, will directly affect the number of sales you make, so be sure to pay attention to what I'm about to reveal to you.

How to Market Yourself as a Seller and Beat the Competition

EBay has no limit. This is because of the diverse variety of products and items available to you, and millions of other buyers and sellers. However, eBay's growing marketplace comes with a few challenges for sellers. For the seller, the most common challenge is;

"How do I stand out from other eBay sellers who sell items similar to mine?"

The answer is easy: market your business. The following are tips on how to market yourself as a seller, as well as beat the competition;

Branding

When I say branding, I mean building an identity and giving your customers something different and unique. For example, if you are selling portable battery fans that are supplied to you from China, put a logo on it to make it your own.

Create a profile and use a consistent pattern of colours for easy identification, and use that profile to talk about your motto, your personal interests and so on. More important than logos and colours, the main part of branding you want to focus on is your *brand-image* and what that image communicates to your customers. What does your business believe in, and do your customers understand your vision?

(Visit: http://pages.ebay.com/help/account/profile.html to find out more)

An image can be the specific way you deal with customers, the quality of your products, the efficiency of your service, how quickly you reply to their queries and the way you approach customer-service. All these things create a **brand-image** in a customer's mind, and moulds the way they view your business.

So, make sure you aim to create the best possible image from the beginning. Ask yourself...

"How do I want my business to be perceived?"

"What can I do to portray myself in that way?"

"What can I do better than my competition?"

"What does my target market want?"

"What would I want as a customer?"

Answering questions like these will allow you to stand tall above the competition and become a respected seller in your niche. On the other hand, without proper business branding, you are just another anonymous eBay seller.

I will also add that, if you are serious about building a brand and establishing a long-term business, you must have an online presence. That is either through a blog or a well-designed website.

Today, a website is much more than just a web-page, it is the face of a business.

The good thing is that anyone can create a website for just a few dollars, by using platforms that are already pre-built with thousands of lay-outs and themes to choose from. In my opinion, the best platform is 'WordPress', which is very well-built, easy to use (with some guidance), and will enable you to create a website like the pros effortlessly. All you need is a bit of assistance to lead you through the steps and to help you create an astonishing, professional and functional website your visitors will admire.

Even better news is that I have actually written a book on the topic, which has already helped many people and will now help you establish your online presence. If you are thinking it is complicated, or a huge effort to create a website, forget about that. This best-selling book was created to make the process easy and painless.

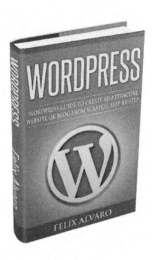

The book is called ***WordPress: Simple WordPress Guide to Create an Attractive Website or Blog from Scratch, step-by-step*** and at the time this book was written, it was ranked as the **#1** book for Web-Site Design and Transformations out of the entire Amazon Kindle store.

The Book is a high-quality quick read, that runs you through all you need to know to create a website or blog step-by-step.

Having a website should be a priority for any business.

Nowadays, when someone hears about a company they are unfamiliar with, the first thing they do is look for them online. A website is your business-card that shows customers that you are established and can be trusted. For you, it will also mean that you will have the means to sell your eBay products on your own site, therefore bringing in more revenue and greater exposure. On top of that, customers will be able to find your shop easily when doing a search on Google or other search engines. The benefits are endless.

Make that investment today. and visit: http://amzn.to/1VHtxZi to order your copy now.

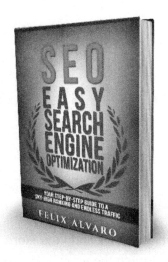

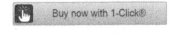

Marketing

Marketing is getting your name out there. Letting people know that you exist and that you have something of value to give them. There are a few methods you can use to market your business and some of those methods are a little bit more advanced, so go with what you feel more comfortable with:

EBay Commerce Network

This merchant Program allows your products and your store to be advertised directly to customers through the use of ad placements on major websites such as; Bing, TheFind, Shopping.com, CNet and many others. To enrol you simply sign up here:
https://merchant.ebaycommercenetwork.com/public/#/public/enroll

and then you place funds for a campaign using PayPal. You will then be charged on a per-click basis, meaning that for every

person that clicks on the ad, you will be a charged a certain fee. To find out more visit:
http://ebaycommercenetwork.com/merchants

Facebook Ads

Facebook Ads is a very powerful tool. They allow you to advertise directly to a specific demographic of consumers, in a particular area and with particular interests. Ensure that you take a good amount of time to think about the consumer of the products you are selling. I would ask three questions to make identification easier;

Firstly; "Who is my customer?" (age, income, gender etc.)

Secondly; "What do they like?"

Finally; "What turns them off?".

Answer those questions and you will have a clearer understanding of how to reach your target market. (Find out more about FB ads by visiting here: https://www.facebook.com/business/products/ads).

Blogs and Forums

There are a few ways you can use blogs and forums. Firstly, ensure that you are part of all the eBay forums and blogs that are relevant to the products you sell and, where your target customers would engage. Secondly, also aim to engage in all relevant forums outside eBay. You can visit forums where people ask questions about certain topics and there you can provide assistance, as well as recommend your product.

Another way is through blog posts on your own website. You can answer questions people have and also write informative posts and guides that provide advice and quality information. You can then simply recommend products and have links to your store.

Cross Promote

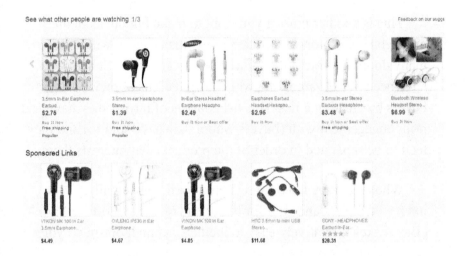

Another no-cost, but very powerful way to advertise is through cross promoting. Your relevant products will appear on other eBayers' listings and their products on your listings. Products will also appear after a customer has checked-out, in relevant search pages, in *My eBay*, emails sent to buyers (if the products they bought is unavailable) and as a recommendation for the item they are viewing.

This increase of exposure can have a massive boost on your sales and on-top of that eBay allows you to choose the 'rules' for the promotion. It lets you to select the type of customers you want to target, making it even more effective. (Find out more here: http://pages.ebay.com/stores/cross-promotions/tutorial/2.html).

Mailing List

This is another must if you want to make big bucks in the online business world. Period. Setting this up early will open many doors for you in the future, far beyond eBay. Sellers who have been in the game for a while keep records of their past buyers by creating a list. This list consists of buyers they have had prior engagement with (buyers whom they have sold to) and they tend to be separated in order of the products that interests them.

Whenever they have a new item to sell, they email all interested buyers and wait for the orders to arrive. Fortunately, eBay makes it relatively easy to include an email opt-in on your shop. They also allow you to create three or more different mailing lists that may target different product categories or consumers, like the pros do.

Another way you can make use of this strategy is through the use of your website (I hope you are starting to understand how essential this is now). You can have people who read your blog posts, customers, people who ask questions and anyone that visits your page for whatever reason, enter their email-address. Doing this step here will allow you to have a list of people that already love what you do, you just send them what they are interested in and there you have a loyal customer for years to come. This will also help with the brand, as you can use your logo and your brand colours in all your newsletter and emails. Take this step seriously.

Get Reviews

Feedback ratings ⓘ

★★★★★	10,466	Item as described	🔵 12,271	🔵 164	🔴 175
★★★★★	11,288	Communication	Positive	Neutral	Negative
★★★★★	10,436	Shipping time			
★★★★★	11,405	Shipping charges		Feedback from the last 12 months	

Like I mentioned earlier, when you are starting out, you should really focus on getting positive feedback from your customers. EBay accounts with positive reviews tend to attract more sales, and this is because online buyers view positive reviews as a vote of confidence on a seller.

In the mind of a buyer, more reviews that are positive, directly translate into trust. Use this to your advantage. Obviously, to get positive feedback you must give a quality service to your customers, there is no way around it. That's why I advise you to implement that from the beginning. Of course, you can't be perfect. But aim to be.

How to Get More Reviews:

However, I know that sometimes no matter how good your service is, people just won't bother to give feedback and reviews. Humans get more excited about complaining, in-comparison to leaving positive feedback. So, this is where you have to be smart and remind people to review you. Here are some tips to help you get more reviews;

Tip#1: Ask

I am sure you have heard the saying:

"If you don't ask, you don't get…"

That is so true! The best way to get more reviews is to simply ask your customers for one. Not all consumers understand the importance of reviews to the seller and as obvious as it sounds, a lot of sellers don't even ask. Make sure that you are not one of those people and ask for a review at every opportunity you get; on your website, any emails you send customers etc.

Tip#2: Make Leaving a Review Easy

I repeat: People are not as motivated to leave positive feedback, as they are to leave negative feedback, so it is your job to make it as easy as possible for them to give you those good reviews. The best way is by integrating direct links to your review profile, from all different places such as newsletters, email follow ups and a website. By doing this, you can make it easier for customers and at the same time, use it as a reminder.

Brilliant. You are gaining great skills that will definitely give you a significant advantage over other sellers. Marketing and branding yourself is essential for you to build a profitable business. As I have showed you in this chapter, it is quite simple and reasonably inexpensive to do. It is now time to take things even one step further. In the next chapter, you will learn how to scale up your business and how to take things to another level. The final chapter is going to be short, but mighty. The information I am about to tell you is essential, so stay focused. You are doing great!

Chapter Six: Take Your Income to The Next Level

You should now have enough information to build a profitable eBay business. In this final chapter, I will show you a few tricks that can allow you to take a small online business to new heights.

Virtual Assistants

This is a killer strategy. If your aim is to build a business that doesn't really need you there physically 24/7 for it to operate, then outsourcing is a must for you. With this strategy, you can actually hire native English speakers from different parts of the world, to manage time-consuming areas of your business inexpensively. These assistants can assist you with various things such as;

- Dealing with customer issues
- Replying to emails
- Taking care of paper work
- Answering phones calls
- And all other day-to-day tasks.

This will not only allow you to focus on more crucial areas of your business, but will also give you more freedom. I mean, what's the point of making a lot of money if you don't have the time to enjoy it? Hiring an assistant will allow you to get closer to the 'financial freedom' many dream of.

However, I wouldn't recommend outsourcing immediately. It is best to first of all learn how to run the business and get some experience so you are able to provide them with the best instructions. When you are ready, one of my favourite websites to find assistants is UpWork.com.

They have thousands of people that you can hire on an hourly basis or at a set price to be your personal assistant. All you do is post a 'job' describing the tasks, and required skills and time. Then you simply choose the best person out of all the applicants. Also, be sure to read their profiles, check their reviews and carry out a thorough interview before hiring them to make sure you get the best person for the task.

Automation Software

Now if you don't want to start outsourcing just yet, there are a few tools you can use to make things run smoother. One of those tools is eBay's own *Selling Manager*.

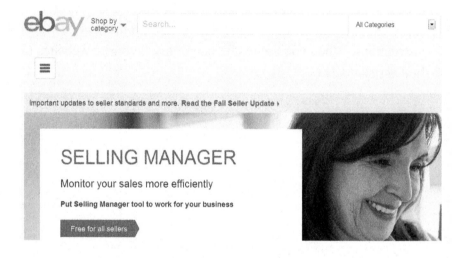

This little tool will allow you stay on top of your business by helping you;

- Easily create lists in bulk using templates or from scratch
- View all your items' status (sold, unsold, active etc.)
- Keep track of your orders
- Export order data
- Print invoices
- Print shipping labels

- Communicate with your customers
- Monitor your customer feedback
- View your sales reports and much, much more!

This free tool is a must if you want to manage all areas of your business yourself. However, if you later-on decide to hire an assistant, all you would have to do is teach them how to correctly manage everything through the Selling Manager and they should be ready to go. (Read more about this tool Here: http://pages.ebay.com/sellerinformation/build-your-business-online/boost-profits/selling-tools/selling-manager.html).

Drop Shipping

I briefly mentioned this earlier, but this is another great strategy that can allow you to automate your business. In a nutshell, drop-shipping will allow you to have a system in place where products move from the supplier directly to the customer without ever touching your hands.

This means that you won't have to store any product and you also won't have to deal with shipping or any returns (still include the information in your listing). All you would be required to do is monitor the sales, make sure that customers receive their products on time, and also that products are delivered safely, and are maintaining high quality.

I would also like to add that many people use this strategy to start their online business with very little investment. They simply set-up the store, and every time there is an order, the supplier receives the order and takes care of everything else for them. All the seller really does is monitor the operation from afar, and grow the brand and customer base.

Using this strategy, you can build multiple online businesses leveraging the suppliers and if you use virtual assistants, they your work will be very minimal. That right there, ladies and gentlemen, is how you build an automated business that runs with or without you.

However, you have to be very wary of who you do business with. It can be a little challenging to find a trustworthy, reliable and consistent drop-shipper. Make sure you negotiate accordingly and ensure that both parties understand their responsibilities in the partnership, otherwise things will not work-out, customers won't get their items and your business won't move forward. Before deciding, read this:
https://www.shopify.com/guides/dropshipping/understanding-dropshipping

TIP: Get a contract written describing each parties' obligations, commitments and get it signed and stamped by a solicitor.

Be Organized and In-control

Now this is common sense, but a majority of people lack this basic trait. With any business you run, you have to know everything about your operation, at least in the beginning where you are managing it yourself. Now, I am not contradicting myself, or trying to confuse you. It is just necessary that when you do make the decision and begin taking action, be sure to keep track of everything.

Use tools like the Selling Manager, have your own spreadsheets, have everything neat and easily accessible, be on top of your game. This advice is for me as well. Sometimes we get comfortable and want to relax before we should. Don't!

Make the decision to stay focused and dedicate yourself to your business. Even if It is a part-time business, in the hours that you dedicate, give 100% of your attention. Of course, we all make mistakes, just be sure to learn from them and always aim to be better. Your entire life can change if you do this right.

Awesome! Congratulations once more, especially for reading this far down! You should now be fully equipped and with enough fuel to get started, and remember you always have this book as a guide. If you want to do a few more checks before making your mind up, that's fine but please don't be a victim of analysis paralysis. Now is the time to grab online businesses by the horns, so don't delay any further, because success can be yours.

Turn to the next page for a quick recap on what we covered in this book!

Here is a quick recap of what we covered in case you need a refresher on a certain step:

1. You now know why you need to be selling on eBay and what they have in-store for you
2. You now know how to open up your store, as well as how the entire payment process works
3. You learned how to find profitable products and where to source them from
4. You learned how to do an effective listing, following all the requirements
5. You learned how to brand and market your business
6. You also learned how to take your business to new heights through outsourcing and automation
7. You also learned many other tips and tricks!

Before You Go

I hope you have enjoyed this book and have received a lot of valuable and beneficial information.

Continue to invest in your eBay business and continue investing in your knowledge. I would also appreciate your feedback, so please if you enjoyed this book, kindly leave a review on Amazon. You may copy this link to do so http://amzn.to/1Fv6bUx

You can also check out our other books that will teach you a variety of skills. You can find our full library at >> http://amzn.to/1Xxmab2

Finally, you can also send me an email if you have any questions, feedback or just want to say hello! (I do reply!) My email address is; (Felix_Alvaro@mail.com)

I thank you once again and God bless!

Felix Alvaro

Before You Go, Here Are Other Books Our Readers Loved!

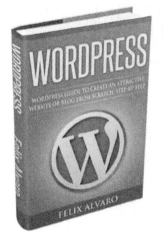

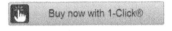 in Web Site Design

Easily Create Your Own Eye-Catching, Professional Website or Blog Using WordPress Today!

Buy now with 1-Click®

 in Functional Analysis

All You Need To Learn To Drive Tons Of Traffic To Your Website Today!

Buy now with 1-Click®

Learn JavaScript Programming Today With This Easy Step-By-Step Guide!

Learn Python Programming Today With This Easy, Step-By-Step Guide!

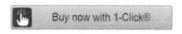

Learn Java Programming
Today With This Easy,
Step-By-Step Guide!

http://amzn.to/1WTgUw0

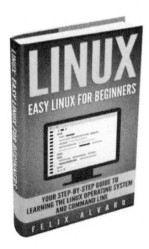

Best Seller in Fiber Optics Engineering

Learn The Linux Operating
System and Command
Line Today!

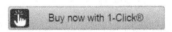

http://amzn.to/1QzQPkY

Learn C Programming Today With This Easy, Step-By-Step Guide

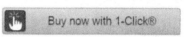

http://amzn.to/1WI6fHu

Learn R Programming With This Easy, Step-By-Step Guide

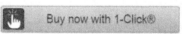

http://amzn.to/24XxoLM

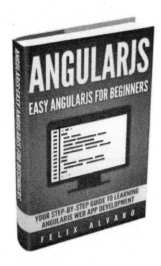

Learn AngularJS
Web-App Developing
Today With This Easy,
Step-By-Step Guide

http://amzn.to/1pDq0BZ

All the best!

Felix Alvaro

CPSIA information can be obtained
at www.ICGtesting.com
Printed in the USA
LVOW05s1614030817
543714LV00012B/1304/P